Just Call Me Mom

Wendy Taylor

Published by Word of Life

Scripture quotations marked NLT are taken from the Holy Bible, New Living Translation, copyright 1996. Used by permission of Tyndale House Publishers, Inc., Wheaton, Illinois 60189. All rights reserved.

All other scripture quotations are taken from the King James Version.

ISBN: 978-0-9782777-0-3

Acknowledgements

First, I would like to give thanks to my Dear Lord and Saviour who opened doors for me to have a rich and fulfilling life. I would also like to thank my husband Glenn who encouraged me to write this book, an endeavour that seemed so overwhelming. I thank God for the partner He gave me to share these many life experiences. Thank you to my son Brent who has continually encouraged me. Thanks to my daughter Alysha and my son-in-law Jon, for your patience and assistance when I so often disappear in my office for hours at a time. Jon your computer skills and advice have been invaluable to me. Karl Kersey, thank you for editing this book and your positive comments, which inspired me.

Introduction

When children were placed into our home, we were very aware that they were leaving their mom and dad, brothers and sisters, and all that was familiar to them. I saw myself filling the void. That emptiness was for a mother. Sometimes this relationship would stretch into weeks, months, or years. Nevertheless, I enjoyed and learned from this role. The one-hundred-plus children that my husband and I were called on to parent, love and care for, were often emotionally scarred, abandoned, and abused. Through the grace of God, we had a wonderful opportunity to show and teach them love, trust, and respect. As you will see in this book, it was not without a price. We found that the pain and suffering that we endured through this whole experience was nothing in comparison to what we received back.

I pray the golden thread of God's goodness and power would shine through as a bright light in the midst of dark and hopeless looking.

Be encouraged dear reader there is nothing too difficult for God.

Jeremiah 32:27 "Behold, I am the LORD, the God of all flesh: is there any thing too hard for me?"

Wendy Taylor

Chapter 1

New Beginnings

"I'm ready for a career change and I think I know what God is calling us to do." These words were unsettling coming from a husband, especially when I was the wife! You see, my dream was to have a peaceful life with a couple of children, a white picket fence, a husband making a good income, living near my mother and father and sisters, and just being happy. It sounded reasonable to me.

Glenn proceeded to tell me that he felt the Lord was leading him to work with children on a full time basis. What helped him arrive at this conclusion was that he had a boy's club in our town that was proving to be very successful. He would pick up the boys in town that hung around the local pool hall and then take them to the school gym. The one boys club had now multiplied into three boys clubs, in various schools throughout the county. During this time, he would play basketball then have a Bible story time with the boys. There were several opportunities to listen to the boys, and he would try to instil positive values whenever the occasion arose. He found this so fulfilling, that his truck-driving career paled in comparison. As he prayed about this, he grew more excited about a career change and especially the idea of working with children on a full-time basis. When he shared his plan with me, I made it clear to him that if God called a couple into the mission field, he would call them both. Furthermore, I knew he hadn't called me. It wasn't that I didn't want God's will in my life. It was just that I truly did not feel called to working with children. I was quite content with my nursing career, as I had graduated a Registered Nursing Assistant, not too many years before.

We talked about this decision at some length, and I realized that my husband was very content with it. On the other hand, I was getting quite distraught that he did not see things my way. We agreed to pray about this. Inwardly I knew that this was not a realistic plan because, after all, I was a nurse and he was a truck driver. We had no training with children so I was quite sure that this would not get very far.

It was only about a week later that we received a phone call from a man by the name of Jack Wall. He sounded very nervous on the phone as he proceeded to tell me he had received our names from someone. They had told him about the boys' clubs Glenn had begun. He wondered if we would consider coming to work for him at his treatment program called Ausable Springs Ranch. There were a number of group homes in his organization, and he had a need for group home parents. I listened to him say that he wanted us to come to Kitchener and live in a large farmhouse where they would place six teen-age boys with us. When I shared this information with my husband, he became so excited! He felt instantly this was the Lord answering his prayers. I was just as sure it wasn't. After all, we were both twenty-four years of age and the boys ranged from twelve to sixteen. I never wanted to live on a farm, and we were still adjusting to married life since we had only been married for two years. I was content living near my parents and had come to enjoy the various Christian friends we had made. It seemed perfectly reasonable to me that this could not possibly be God's will for us. My husband would not give up on the idea, so before I knew what had happened, Glenn arranged for both of us to go and look at the farm, and get an overview of the program.

While traveling to Kitchener, I had butterflies in my stomach. As I looked around at the beautiful rolling hills, they brought peace to my heart, and I became mindful of the Creator who had my future mapped out. He had promised never to leave me or forsake me.

Jake, the director, proved to be a very easy guy to talk to. He explained to us that we would be relief parents at first, moving into five different group homes for one week at a time, giving relief to the foster parents. If we wanted to have a group home in the future, they would be open to this as well.

The ride home proved to be very quiet as we both contemplated what changes this move would make, if we decided to go through with it. The more I thought about this, the more convinced I was that this was not for us.

We knew we had to come to a unified decision. We agreed to pray about this for the weekend, and we hoped to come to an agreement. The more we talked and prayed the angrier I became and the more peaceful my husband became. The deadline was Sunday evening and we would need to give our answer. The thing that bothered me so much was that my husband looked so happy and at peace! I, on the other hand, was angry and confused. Finally, by Saturday evening, I realized that I needed to surrender my will to God and depend on Him to give us direction. I told God if He showed me clearly that we were to go, I would be willing.

The next morning as we were getting ready to go to church, a choir was singing on a program we regularly watched on TV. My husband called me into the room and told me to sit down for a minute. I watched for a moment when suddenly the screen went blank and writing appeared across the screen! 1 John 3:17 (NLT) "If someone has enough money to live well and sees a brother or sister in need but shows no compassion - how can God's love be in that person?" When I finished reading, the verse went off the screen and the choir started singing again.

I broke down and started crying. I felt God had spoken to me. I said to my husband, "Let's call and say we are going." By this time in my life, I knew God's plans were always better than my plans in the end. After all, He had created me for a plan and a purpose. Why try life my way, when he had the master plan and knew best?

We thought, prayed, and talked about how this decision would change our lives, but little did we know. In the Old Testament, Gideon had used a wool fleece to test God's will in Judges Chapter 6. We decided to put out three fleeces to make sure we were on the right track.

The first fleece was our desire to travel to the west coast for a month. Would the director allow us to start a month later than he planned? He agreed and that settled the matter.

The second fleece was finding somewhere to store our furniture free. We knew this was quite a request, but it wasn't long before Ted Willms a friend of ours, offered us a room in his warehouse where we could store our furniture at no cost.

The third fleece was Glenn being able to sell his truck. He had a rather large truck that he used for business, and would have no need for it now. One day after church, we came home and found a man on our porch waiting for us. He asked if he could buy the truck. My husband offered to let him take it for a drive. He said it wasn't necessary. Before we knew what was happening he counted out the cash and left with the keys to his new truck. When the third fleece was answered, we were surer than ever that God was directing us. We had a great peace in our hearts that sealed our plans for the future.

What a life changing adventure we were about to embark on! Unknown to us, it would last for twenty-five years.

Chapter 2

Lessons to Learn

It was a beautiful day and today my life would change forever. The sun was shining and it was time to get our belongings in the car and head up to Kitchener and our new home. Joannie and Neil, my sister and brother-in-law traveled in a car behind us to give us moral support.

As we traveled down the busy highway, I was deep in thought about promises I had read in the Bible. I had found out recently that I could not have children. When I had cried and prayed about this, I found a Bible verse: Psalm 113:9 "He maketh the barren woman to keep house, and to be a joyful mother of children. Praise ye the Lord." I felt this promise was for me from God, and that he would fulfill his plan in my life. I did know that He had given me a great love for children, and that somehow the direction of my life would be with children. We finally pulled up to the little apartment where we would be staying. The new key was waiting for us. My mouth dropped open as I looked around at the filthy apartment full of mouse dirt, a filthy fridge, and stove and the odour seemed unhealthy. I felt overwhelmed and tired. I sat on the corner of the dirty bed in the corner of the room and the tears began to flow. My sister tried to comfort me as we cleaned and unpacked. It was a rough beginning!

It was time to meet our first charges. We drove down the winding driveway to a large farmhouse nestled between the many trees. Henry and Jane were the group home parents that were going away for their week off. Henry met us at the door with a broken arm that was in a sling. He welcomed us but we barely got in the door when we felt a tension mounting, and could hear fighting in the other room. He went on to explain that his arm broke when it went through the window, while he was chasing one of the boys. Henry told us the boys were very hyperactive, and he hoped they would settle down for us. About a half hour later, Henry and Jane were waving goodbye to us, telling us they would be back in a week. We called the boys together, and told everyone to take a seat. We looked into their sullen faces, and saw six very angry boys, who felt they had once again been abandoned to strangers. I was terrified, but my husband was relaxed and confident. One of the things we were told was that it was better to begin tough, because you can always lighten up later, but it is very hard to do the reverse. We spelled out the rules to them clearly and much to our surprise, they began to look more comfortable. We wanted to help them, and so we knew that we needed to be strict or we wouldn't be able to influence their lives in a positive way. We truly felt a love in our hearts for these boys, and we knew it was from God. We felt as though we could see the pain in their hearts.

We were grateful to be here, but after the emotionally charged evening we just had, it was not hard to fall asleep that night, even if it was in a new bed. My husband awoke to a strange sound in the middle of the night. He got out of bed and tiptoed into the room where the noise was coming from. There he found David on his crutches urinating out the screen window. This explained why there was such a foul smell coming from that room. Because he had broken his leg, and it was difficult getting to the bathroom, a can was left beside the bed. It was left there for his convenience, but he had decided this was more fun.

The next day was eventful as well. My husband was learning that if the boys were quiet, it usually spelled trouble. Rex had disappeared for a long time. Glenn quietly went up the stairs and quickly opened the door. He found the surprise approach to be best. He found Rex with a shocked look on his face clamouring to get his suitcase under the bed. When Glenn asked Rex for the suitcase, he begged Glenn not to look in it. Glenn knew then that he needed to see what was in the suitcase, to find out what would cause such a terrified look on Rex's face. When Glenn opened the suitcase, he found forty pairs of panties in it. Rex admitted he had been stealing panties from the group homes and foster homes he had been in, and would try them on and fantasize in them. Consequences followed and the panties were disposed of.

It took a while to get used to locking the bedroom door and never leaving my keys, purse, jewellery, or change lying around because it could be stolen. It would then find its way to a pawnshop. More than one foster parent's rings had been stolen and pawned off. Getting up in the middle of the night was even tricky. You never knew who was lurking around in the hallway by the bathroom. My husband usually escorted me if I had to get up, and I made sure I was properly covered.

I found out very early on in this new life, that my husband was a natural with the boys. He was firm but could also have fun with them. They had a lot of respect for him. I found it very comfortable to hide behind my husband because he was very protective of me. This worked out fine at first. He handled all the discipline problems, and I concentrated on becoming friends with our new charges. Since I enjoy baking and cooking, I would often bake cookies and special treats for their lunches. I felt this would give me brownie points with them. I also would play table games with them, and was a good listener when they wanted to share their hearts.

One morning, my husband went out to a meeting and I was left at the breakfast table with the boys. The first fifteen minutes went by uneventfully. Suddenly, one of the boys poked another boy and a fight broke out. Tempers were flaring and it wasn't long before the whole group was enraged. Their voices were growing louder, language was deteriorating quickly, and my commands to settle down went unheard. Thankfully, it wasn't long before my husband came home and calmed the household down. I found out at that moment that what I was doing wasn't working. Putting candies and cookies in their lunches wasn't enough. To win their respect, I had to change my ways. I had a lot of learning to do. Thankfully, we had several days a month where we took training classes from psychologists on techniques in dealing with behavioural issues. Because our children had been traumatized in some way, they were emotionally wounded or disturbed. Many of them had been abused or neglected.

We found that by using behaviour modification along with natural, logical consequences that it was quite amazing what could be accomplished with just a few simple techniques. We found that if a child misbehaved, it was best to give a quick but powerful consequence that would be over that same day. As an example, it worked best to take away all privileges such as TV, radio, telephone, and snack then have an early bedtime. The next morning we would forgive and begin a new day. If the consequences dragged on for a length of time, the foster parent would begin to pay. The child would get discouraged and try to retaliate. Threatening a child with a more severe consequence than you are willing to enforce, makes the child not believe you next time.

One of the first boys we had in the group home was a boy by the name of Wayne. He was hyperactive, impulsive, and very difficult. We spent time alone with Wayne, reassuring him that we loved him and that he was special. By the end of the week, we had built a relationship with him. He didn't want us to leave. It felt so good to think we were making a difference in at least one life.

Quite often Glenn would take the boys horseback riding. He found they were all very independent and wanted to saddle their own horses. Glenn always offered to tighten the cinches on the horses, but Kenny wanted to tighten his own. Kenny had the smallest horse, a Shetland pony. The horses were quite clever. They would fill their bellies with air so the cinch would not be so tight. This is what happened to Kenny's pony. Glenn led the group down the trail, all six boys galloping behind him. Suddenly he heard someone yelling behind him. He turned to look. There was Kenny sliding off the side of the pony, as it dragged him by his leg, caught in the stirrups. The dust was flying and everyone came to a halt to try to rescue Kenny. Nothing seemed broken or too bruised other than his pride.

Chapter 3

Never a Dull Moment

Our week was up at the previous home and it was time to move on to relieve our next group home parents. Gerald and Sidney were ready for a week off. By the looks of the six angry faces looking at us, we determined that the boys were not too happy about it. It was always such an adjustment for the boys to be left in someone else's charge, especially someone they did not know.

We had an evening talk with them, introducing ourselves and trying to get them to share a little as well. Then we went on to explain that one of the things we did with every group home we did relief for, was to have a Bible story and prayer time. We noticed an uncomfortable atmosphere in the room almost immediately. We started out by asking, "Does anyone know what the true meaning of Christmas and Easter are?" No one knew, although there were a few guesses like the Easter Bunny and Santa Claus. We then asked, "Have any of you been to church or Sunday School?" A few boys remembered they had gone as very small children but couldn't really remember anything. By asking these questions, we were trying to get a feel for how much they knew and where to start. It was obvious that we had to start from the beginning.

After Bible study, we were confident we were off to a good start, as the boys responded more positively than we had imagined. It was time to get comfortable in a new bed in a different home once again. Before falling asleep, we prayed together for God's blessing on this home and each of the boys, that the seed of God's word would fall on fertile ground in the boy's hearts.

I awoke to my husband shaking my arm and whispering "Shh!" I listened to footsteps on the stairs as hushed voices were whispering outside of our room. When things got quiet, my husband jumped out of bed. He hurried up the long staircase taking the stairs two at a time. He glanced in the bedrooms and saw six boys in their beds with their covers over them looking like angels. Something wasn't right, so he went to the first bed and pulled the covers back and found Gerry lying there like a soldier and completely dressed with shoes on. He proceeded to do the same to the other five boys with the same results. After questioning the boys individually, we had found out quickly never to interrogate them together. It was too easy to stick with one lie. When questioning them apart we would get many versions of the same incident. We would then piece the truth together. We finally concluded we had the closest to the truth that we would be getting. They had stolen the cupcakes I had baked that evening, along with most of the snack foods that were to last an entire week. They planned on having a party, running down the fire escape, and playing tag outside. After hearing the story Glenn felt his temper rising and knew he needed to pull away from the situation for a few moments. He told them he would be back in ten minutes. He needed a little time to cool off, and think about an appropriate consequence. We talked and thought about how to handle this. We knew we were being tested. The way we handled this, would determine the way the rest of the week would go. We decided that since they were so energetic, they needed to get tired. Glenn had them follow him to the barn where they were each given a shovel. Glenn said, "Shovel the manure out of this barn for the remainder of the night if any of you are found slacking off I will baptize you in the horse trough." Being filled with cold water, it didn't look too inviting. He went to bed for a couple of hours. When morning came, he went out to check on the boys. They had, surprisingly enough, accomplished a lot. We had six very tired boys who slept most of the day. After that, we never had a problem with them partying while we were sleeping.

A few days later, my husband and the boys went out to rake leaves. This was such a beautiful fall day that we were sure it would be a perfect day.

Davis was in the house with me, finishing his house chore before he went out to rake. When he finished vacuuming the living room carpet, I went to inspect the job. I called him back and told him he would have to do it again. He got a very angry look in his eyes and walked toward the closet. The next thing I knew, he was pointing a .22 rifle at me. He said, "I'm going to blow your head off!"

I calmly told him, "Put the gun away, go outside and play, and I won't tell Glenn." I did not know if the gun was loaded, since we were at someone else's home. Almost immediately, after I said that, I knew I had made a mistake. I would have to tell my husband. That night after we were in bed trying to settle down, after another hectic day with the boys, I told my husband about the events of the day. Before I knew it, he was running up the stairs two at a time to straighten out Davis. He gave him a very firm talking to. He told Davis, "Young man there is something you need to understand, Wendy is my wife and as long as I am here you won't be threatening her or hurting her." The next morning,

Davis had extra chores and we watched him more closely. I felt bad that I had broken my word to Davis, but I feel I did the right thing in telling my husband because it was important for the boys to get the message that my husband would stand behind me at all times. Many of our boys had little respect for women because they had witnessed their moms beaten and abused by boyfriends or husbands. They needed to see my husband in the role of my protector.

About a week later, Davis stole his foster parent's car and drove it down the 401, a local four-lane highway. He was only ten years old and too short to see over the dash so he sat on his knees and his foster brother sat on the floor working the clutch, gas, and brakes. They drove about twenty miles like this before the police pulled them over.

There were many times we sat with the boys individually and listened to them share their pain and heartaches. It was at these times we would introduce them to our greatest friend, someone that would never leave them or forsake them - Jesus Christ. It was so honouring for us to have them excited about us coming to relieve their foster parents. Many evenings were spent playing table games with them. It took me a while to understand why they always wanted me to sit in a certain chair. After losing almost every game, I finally caught on that they were reading my cards through the reflection in my glasses! It was hard staying two steps ahead of them.

Chapter 4

More Challenges

Raymond and Bessie's home was our next challenge. They were the most experienced of all the couples and consequently had the most difficult children. After getting a report from them regarding their six boys, we waved goodbye and wondered what this next week would hold.

Roger a tall, slim fourteen-year-old youth was a very interesting fellow. He was also the chief aggravator in this home. He was a sensitive, artistic, musical, and creative guy who had very strong feminine qualities. His favourite aggravation that sent the whole house into a wild frenzy was when he would sing in a high voice that sounded like a female opera singer. Before he would begin singing, he would move furniture in front of the door and then would accompany himself at the piano. He would sing as loudly as possible. Within a few minutes you could hear boys running from everywhere in the house wanting to shut him up by whatever means necessary. It became a zoo in that household. We would send all the boys back to their rooms and order Roger to stop the noise. He was usually compliant. After all, he had accomplished his mission by sending the house into an uproar.

Another of Roger's hobbies was traveling. He had a large map on his bedroom wall. He would dream about where he would next like to take a trip. He would pinpoint where he wanted to travel next. He would take a few dollars and a small bag of clothes and away he would go. Hitchhiking became an inexpensive way to travel and even had a few advantages as well.

One beautiful morning, he decided to he wanted to see the Rocky Mountains. Of course, a 2,000-mile trip did not intimidate him. He left with ten dollars in his pocket and a change of clothes. When hitchhiking he would offer to buy lunch for the driver. In every case, the driver would stop to eat and end up paying for him. When he became tired, he would ask to be dropped off at a motel. He would go sit in the waiting room with a newspaper and fall asleep on the couch. If he were awakened by security, he would tell them that he must have fallen asleep reading his newspaper. He would then exit to the hall, until the security left the area. Then he would return and finish his night's sleep. He ate well, slept soundly, and finally arrived in British Columbia. When he arrived, he thought he would travel down into Washington to have a look around. This ended up being his big mistake. The guards were alerted when he did not carry his identification on him. After questioning him, they finally got him to tell them where he was from. We received a phone call saying that they were holding him in jail and they would fly him back to Ontario. Because of his age, they couldn't hold him there for long. He was thrilled to be also getting a plane trip on his little vacation. His foster dad met him at the airport in Toronto. After a very firm talk about the consequences of his trip, it was decided that he would have to work to pay for his plane ticket. The next day Roger disappeared again. This time the goal was to earn money for his plane trip. He started out by visiting the Salvation Army and buying himself a suit and getting a haircut. He had long shoulder-length hair. He got a job waiting tables in a restaurant by lying about his age and experience. He stole the waitresses' tips, and after a week showed up at the house with enough money to pay for his plane ticket! There were consequences once again but I have to admit it was a job staying ahead of this fellow!

He loved to make cookies with me and help me bake. I have to admit I didn't mind a little help in the kitchen as long as the boys washed and had supervision. My husband had a more difficult time accepting Roger. He really had to pray about their relationship. We found, throughout our experiences, that when we struggled with acceptance it was the Lord working out something within us. We would ask the Lord to change the kids, but he usually changed us first.

A few days later, Jim created an incident we will never forget. He was a short but stocky twelve-year-old boy who had a beard and very broad shoulders. He took psychotropic medication to calm him down from the violent outbursts he would have. He had pushed his aunt off a bridge and almost killed his grandmother by pushing her down the stairs. One of the boys came up to report to us that Jim was very angry and was tearing up his room. Glenn went down to his room to see what the trouble was. Jim had a crazed look in his eyes. He was flinging a pair of ice skates back and forth so no one could get near him. His other hand was pouring a bottle of pills down his throat. Glenn reached out to grab the pills and the skate hit Glenn's lip. Blood started trickling down his chin and he yelled for me to bring the boys upstairs. The whole house was bordering on hysteria by this time. I phoned the hospital and an ambulance came and took Jim to the hospital where they tied him to the stretcher and were able to pump his stomach before it got into his blood stream. As I retreated to my room that evening, the Lord reassured me through his Word that I was safe in his arms, and that he loved me.

Chapter 5

A Home of Our Own

After bouncing from home to home for about six months, we decided to request our own group home. We were given a large farmhouse about ten miles to the closest store. It had six bedrooms and two bathrooms. For a farmhouse, it was a beautiful old home with a lot of character. We had a large farm kitchen where the eight of us could sit around the kitchen table comfortably. A large dinner bell sat on the top of the house that would come in very handy to call everyone in for supper. A large veranda encompassed two sides of the house. My relaxation often took place out here. With our two dogs at my feet, I would curl up and read a good book. Surrounding our home were beautiful rolling hills, where cows grazed contentedly. The spring was my favourite time of the year, when newborn calves followed their mothers. It usually was obvious which calf belonged to which mother. I would often think, I wonder how God feels when he looks down and sees these cows taking better care of their young than many humans do. We had firsthand knowledge of this with so many abused and fragmented children coming to live with us.

Our sprawling 100-acre farm was an excellent location for our family of six boys between the ages of twelve and sixteen years. We felt, what better setting for our boys. They would have to go a long way to get into serious trouble. Running away would not be as tempting either. After all, what could happen in such a peaceful setting? We were about to find out!

One beautiful crisp January day, all the boys were out tobogganing on the snow-laden hills. The snow was glistening in the bright sun and it seemed like a perfect winter day. As it drew closer to supper, it was time to ring the dinner bell. I rang the bell, which usually brought six hungry boys scrambling to the table. I rang it again. There was still no response. A sick feeling started to develop in my stomach. Something was wrong! Suddenly the phone rang and someone at the other end of the line was asking me if I knew anything about a robbery that had taken place at the other end of the lane. They said there were six pairs of footprints in the newly fallen snow, leading up to the house. The caller was asking, "Could it be your boys?" I told her it was most likely them, since they were all missing.

Glenn and I ventured out in the car with our flashlight like two detectives. The snowflakes were coming down, leaving a beautiful golden hue around the streetlights. What a breathtaking sight. It would have been a perfect night except for our mission. We were following six pairs of footprints sliding along the side of the road. They slid down all the small hills along the way appearing to be having the time of their lives! We drove along, cautiously watching for our boys, when suddenly we saw a store in the distance. Sure enough, the footprints led right up to the store. We went in, and asked the storekeeper if he had seen six boys in the last while. He told us they had stopped to buy cigarettes, and they had been in the store just ten minutes earlier. We continued until we saw six frozen looking boys hitchhiking. We pulled over and Glenn said with his most authoritative voice, "Get in boys." Without any resistance, they piled into our station wagon. We found out that they had gone to the neighbour's house to see if the neighbours were home. If they were, they would ask what time it was. After ringing the doorbell and hearing the dog barking in the other room and no one coming to the door, they surmised that no one was home and the dog was confined. They went around the back of the house looking for an open window. When they saw a window cracked open, one of the boys shimmied up a tree and climbed through the bedroom window. He ran down and opened the door for the others. After ransacking the bedrooms, they searched the house and found a rare old coin collection under the Christmas tree. They filled their pockets with rare old coins and ventured out to the store to buy cigarettes. They threw the oddly shaped, and more valuable, coins in the snow on the side of the road that they thought the storeowner wouldn't take.

After interviewing each boy separately to discover the truth, we took them back to the owner of the coin collection and had them apologize. The couple was so gracious and understanding. The boys chopped wood for the family for several weeks for payment. Most of the coins were never recovered. The love and forgiveness this couple displayed reminded me of the love Christ had for us when he paid the debt for our sin, dying on that cruel cross, while we were sinners. The difference is all we have to do is ask forgiveness and the debt is paid. There is no way we can recompense for our sin.

Chapter 6

Clean at Last

Each night we continued to have a Bible story and prayer time with the boys. We found this was one of the most valuable times of the day. Often hurts and secrets, from past abuses, they had carried far too long were exposed at this time.

One evening, after explaining to the boys that God had a wonderful plan for their lives, and that all they had to do was ask forgiveness and surrender to God, something remarkable happened. Tim was a fourteen-year-old boy who used to have the problem of running away whenever he was troubled. He was quite a likable boy, and within a short time settled down and became very comfortable with us. The running stopped and we knew we were making headway. His biggest problem was that he had trouble sharing his feelings with anyone. Following our talk and prayer time, we observed that he was hanging around, as if he wanted to talk to us. After the last boy headed up to bed, he asked if he could talk to us. We said, "Of course Tim, what's on your mind?"

He said, "I don't know how to say this, but I want to be a Christian." We explained to him that Jesus died for his sins and that all he had to do was ask forgiveness and accept Jesus as his personal Saviour and he would be reborn into God's family. He prayed after Glenn and when the prayer ended, he started to laugh. We looked at each other wondering if this was a trick, or had he conned us? Glenn asked, "Tim, what are you laughing about?" He responded," I feel so clean inside it tickles. I have never felt like this before."

We knew that his sins had truly been forgiven and it was a joy to see a new babe born into God's kingdom. We assured him that the angels were having a party in heaven celebrating that he had been brought into God's family.

Glenn and I shared the meal preparation at our group home. Baking cookies, desserts, and most of the other cooking was my responsibility. Glenn had several things he would cook that were his specialty. It would give me a break so I didn't mind. It was like cooking for an army. These growing boys had tremendous appetites. Glenn even took up baking bread with great success.

My husband loved to experiment with different kinds of foods. One day he and the boys told me to stay out of the kitchen, while they prepared the entire meal! It wasn't long that they called me to supper with big grins on their faces. I had a feeling I wasn't going to like their surprise. Sure enough, the meal consisted of dandelion greens and a groundhog that they had baked in the oven. They had so much fun preparing this with Glenn. They told me they would not tell me what it was until I took a bite. I gingerly took a bite and they all laughed hysterically. They announced that Glenn had shot a couple of groundhogs that afternoon and they cleaned and prepared them and then roasted them. They smacked their lips, and cleaned up every bite, as they bragged about how good it was. I still wonder if they really enjoyed it. Funny thing is they never had groundhog again.

We had many meetings with the boys' parents along with their social workers. One that stands out in my mind was a fifteen-year-old by the name of Phillip. He had sexually assaulted a three-year-old baby girl, so he was placed in our home. He was mentally challenged. He was very mild mannered and you would think him harmless. When I had read his report, I have to admit that I had a very hard time accepting him and being his mom. I had a little talk with God again, this time telling him he had better move Phillip, because he was one child I could not love. I knew if I were to have any positive effect on his life I would need to change my attitude. The problem was I didn't really want to change it, and furthermore I felt this was asking too much of me. After all, I didn't feel he deserved my love and forgiveness! God reminded me that if he could forgive Phillip, who was I to hang on to this crime and hold back my forgiveness. I asked God to change my heart and help me. A strange thing happened. I started to see the pain in his heart, and God did change my attitude toward him.

The social worker decided it was high time that Phillip found out a family secret that had been kept from him all of his life. We all sat around the room, Phillip, his parents, his social worker, and Glenn and I. His mother told him that his dad was not his real dad. Tears began to run down Phillip's face as he began to realize why he had always been rejected by his stepdad. He looked at his family and said, "Why didn't you tell me?" They all sat there not knowing how to answer, as the social worker tried to give an explanation the best she could. As he sat there with tears streaming down his face I knew he needed his mom to run over and give him a hug and reassure him of her love. It didn't happen. There was a cold silence, as my heart broke for this young man. I knew my hug could never substitute at this moment, for the hug he needed from his mom.

Chapter 7

More Excitement

One day my husband got the toboggans out and told the boys to have fun tobogganing down the beautiful snow covered hills. He gave them clear instructions to stay away from the treed areas. Kenny was the first to try. He jumped on the sleigh, and at breakneck speed, went down the hill, headed directly for the trees! He came to an abrupt stop when he met a tree head on. He lay on the snow gasping for breath as the troop came running toward him to make sure he was still breathing. After a few minutes, his breath came back to him. One more lesson learned!

That afternoon I had to go over to the office that was next door. When I went in to get more reports, I saw a longhaired youth about sixteen years old sitting there looking very dejected. I went into the director's office and asked who he was. Jake said, "His name is Jerry, he's fifteen years old and he keeps running away. We are getting ready to send him off to a training school because no one can contain him." My heart went out to this young fellow. That night at supper, when I had a few minutes alone with my husband, I asked him if we could take Jerry in. He agreed and said that it depended on the director. When I asked him, he said, "You people already have six very tough kids, are you sure this is what you want?" I assured him we wanted to try it. He told me that if it didn't work, that Jerry would be placed in a training school, which is a lock-up for juvenile offenders. Jerry moved in, and within a very short time, we began to build a relationship with him. He never ran from us, and even ended up accepting the Lord as his Saviour.

Sundays' were always a challenge. With seven boys to have showers and dressed appropriately, it could be very stressful getting everyone ready for church. We wanted the boys to be dressed their best so we purchased suits, ties, and white shirts for them. This was when it was fashionable to wear suits and your best clothes to church. When we arrived to church in our station wagon, the boys would hurry into the church to grab the first row. They thought it was the best seat in the house. We would position ourselves right behind them. This one Sunday I glanced over their shoulders and was alarmed at what I saw. There in front of me and in front of the pastor and everyone on the stage I saw seven pairs of legs crossed, with bare feet showing between their pant legs and their Sunday shoes. I couldn't wait to ask them where everyone's socks were. They informed me later that I didn't have the washing finished and no one had socks to wear. I was one very embarrassed mother!

Another Sunday I saw them all parading out of the church, single file, with orange juice moustaches. That morning we had been in a rush and I did not have time to check everyone's faces. This turned out to be another embarrassing moment.

A lovely older couple attended our church named the Morrisons. I will never forget them inviting our family, all nine of us, over for Sunday dinner. I can't remember what we had to eat but I do remember the kindness they showed us. We had quite a drill in the car about manners before we went in to visit. The boys made us proud the way they conducted themselves.

In the evening as a reward when the boys were trying to please us, we would sometimes take them to the movies, an activity that usually made everyone happy. There wasn't the stress of arguing and fighting. Occasionally we would take a movie in that would not be suitable. It would have too much violence, inappropriate language, or sexual content. We would simply walk out when this occurred. I'm sure we must have made quite a scene when this would happen. We thought it was important for the boys to learn that it was possible to walk out, if we weren't happy with the movie. It also taught them what was appropriate. They were generally not too happy when this occurred but it was a learning lesson.

One morning we woke up to a terrible snowstorm. Everyone was housebound. All of the sudden we had a knock at the door. It was a social worker for one of the children. He told us his car was stuck in a snowbank, and he couldn't move. He wanted to know if he could stay with us until the storm passed. We were happy to put him up for a few days until the road started clearing. That night as we sat around the living room in a circle having our Bible lesson, he had tears in his eyes as he heard the boys pray aloud and pray for their family members. He told us later, that he was touched by the eager responses of the boys, and that this was a stepping-stone to him eventually finding the Lord as his Saviour. That night we heard a whimpering outside our door. There stood a little black dog that was trembling. We let him in and warmed him up with warm milk and blankets. We found out later that this little dog would have terrible seizures. He was one more of God's creatures that needed us. Our family was growing with seven boys, two dogs, chickens, and pigs.

We gave each of the boys a piglet that they would then raise. They were to feed it with the intention of eventually sending it to the market and making a profit. They were told that they should not play with them because they were not pets. In spite of our warnings, they named them and played with them all the time. It was a heartbreaking day when it was time to send the pigs to market.

Chapter 8

No Boredom!

My husband and I felt very blessed that even though every day was a challenge, our home was under control most of the time. Our trainers told us that we were a good combination. Our personalities were very different but together we could supply the tough and tender parenting model, which the kids needed desperately. Occasionally, we would come across couples who had only one attribute or the other, and it usually didn't work. If they were too strict and didn't know how to show love they came across mean, which resulted in the kids either getting very discouraged and eventually giving up trying, or a full blown case of rebellion.

A new couple joined our team of foster parents. They loved everyone in every way. In fact, they didn't know how to be strict. They felt that if they showed the children enough love, the children would respond and behaviours would change. Well the opposite occurred. Their house got more and more out of control, until one day, one of the boys got a hold of a gun and shot out all the windows. The couple, along with their two babies, lay on the floor until the shooting stopped. The foster boys were all outside as this shooting spree took place. No one was hurt but it was a terrifying experience. Another time they had been threatened by one of their boys and they hid all the knives in their house so that neither their children nor they would be harmed. They didn't last long. Our heart went out to them because we knew they had come into this work with the right motives.

It was time for a new boy to move into our home. Most of the boys were in care for about a year but occasionally they would go home sooner. When one would leave, it wasn't long until another would come. The doorbell rang and standing there with his social worker was Kris, an eleven-year-old redheaded freckle faced boy. He had a very angry, hostile look on his face. He no sooner got in the door, than his social worker told us that Kris hated women. Kris sat there listening as the social worker went on to tell us that he had harmed his female schoolteacher, injured his mother, and tried to kill his grandmother. He had been expelled from the school system in Toronto at eleven years old. He was left to run wild and he used to sit in the theatres in the middle of the night and watch adult movies. No one cared. The social worker told us that I was not to be left alone with Kris, because he would try to hurt me as he had every other woman who tried to care for him. When the social worker left, my husband had a very firm talk with Kris. He told him that he had better know Kris would never hurt his wife, or he would have to deal with my husband. I am not sure what Kris was thinking would happen, but he looked shook up. He needed to see that my husband was my protector, not abuser, as he had witnessed in the past. Kris had an extremely vulgar mouth and pulled some of the worst temper tantrums I had ever seen. During these times, my husband would have to restrain him until he would calm down. There was also a soft, sweet side to Kris, which I discovered. He loved to help me in the kitchen, which helped us develop a very close bond. He never did try to hurt me.

Because Kris had never sat down with his family for supper, he didn't have any manners. Eating with him at the supper table was a challenge. He would literally throw his food at his face. When we were having spaghetti with tomato sauce, it was not a pretty picture. We would remind him constantly that he had to use a fork and knife, but to no avail. When he finished eating, he would have the food in his hair, face, clothes, and all around him on the floor. We eventually put a mirror in front of him so he could see what he looked like when he was eating. That helped some. He did eventually learn to eat like a gentleman. When we prayed for the meal, he would always put his hand on his hot food sitting on his dinner plate. He told us he did this because he wanted to make sure it was still there when he opened his eyes.

Humorous, ridiculous, things often happened to me. I know I was the cause of many of these events. I believe God gave me this gift, so I could laugh at myself, to balance the many tears I shed saying goodbye to my children, never seeing most of them again.

It was time for a break. We would often go to my parents for a weekend to be recharged, and to have a little bit of normalcy. One day, my mom and I decided to go to Windsor to do a bit of shopping. We were driving down this one street in Windsor when I noticed everyone waving at us. I remarked to my mom that I had never seen Windsor so friendly. I waved back and gave the drivers a big smile. The truck drivers didn't look too happy with me but I wasn't going to let that stop me! We were rolling along when all of the sudden I saw three lanes of traffic all heading toward me. I was going the wrong way down a one-way street! Right about that time, I noticed this policeman walking toward my car. Now when I see an officer in uniform I seem to get very emotional! I started to laugh the closer he got to my car. I thought it was like watching a movie only I was in it. There I was sitting in my car perched up on the curb. I was laughing hysterically while the policeman was knocking on my window. Eventually I found the handle to put the window down. He asked for my license and ownership. I continued to laugh as I fumbled through my big purse looking for my identification. Finally, I handed it to him. He shook his head and just said, "Wendy I'll hold this traffic up and you get out of here." I was relieved to be going the same direction as the rest of the world!

Chapter 9

Vacation

It was summer and time to think of vacation. We knew that it was going to be very important to keep the boys busy. There was a small lake only several miles from our home and we planned to spend as much time as possible there. One beautiful sunny day we packed the kids up and decided to go on a picnic to our favourite place. Everyone was so excited! I was even talked into going into the water this time. Every time they went swimming, they would beg me to come in as well. I usually refused and would sit on the beach and read with one eye on my boys. This particular day my husband could not go, so I had the whole group to myself. I gave them some last minute instructions that I expected to be obeyed. Anyone not following my rules, would be sitting watching, instead of having fun swimming. There was a floating dock in the middle of this bottomless lake. The boys were all good swimmers and I was not a strong swimmer but I could keep my head above water. The water was refreshing and I managed to get out to the floating dock. Finally, I was ready to swim back to shore. The dock had drifted quite a ways out, but I was confident I could make it. I started to swim towards shore. I got about half way to shore when I realized I had not judged the distance properly and the shore was much further than I had originally thought. I felt panicky as I realized that I was only about half way there, and was too tired to go further. My chest got tight, and I knew I was beginning to panic. I called the boys, and before I knew it, they were all beside me. They wanted to reach out to me, and help me because they could see I was struggling. I told them to just talk to me but don't touch me. I was terrified that I might drown one of them, in my attempts to survive. They swam beside me encouraging me, and finally I could reach bottom and it was such a relief. I am so thankful for my heroes who saved my life.

Since I was the official barber, not because I had any training but because I loved to be creative, I was the one to do the honours when it came to the haircuts. I let the boys decide what type of haircuts they wanted. Some had a very punk look, some had initials carved in the back of their hair, some had it shaved very close to their heads, and some a bowl cut. They decided what they wanted and I did my best to please them. We felt this was one decision that they could make and the consequences of a wrong decision were not too serious, as the hair would grow back within a few weeks.

We thought it would be fun to take the boys on a real trip. The more we talked about it the more our plans started becoming a reality. There was so much planning to do for the camping trip we were planning.

Since it was summer vacation, we thought we would take the boys to Wisconsin. To take a family this size meant a lot of preparation. For grocery shopping my usual two carts full a week would not cut it this time, since we would be doing all the cooking for two weeks. The other group home that was traveling with us also had six boys plus their two small children. In total, we had thirteen boys, two small children, and four adults.

It was finally time to set off on our trip. Our eight-hour trip in the car was not an easy feat. The boys would be obnoxious, and to make it worse they all tried to outdo each other. The other station wagon followed us. It seemed that if one child didn't need to stop and go to the bathroom, another did. Once we stopped at McDonald's and one of the boys ran to the other side of the building. We followed him and wondered why he wasn't heading to the bathroom like everyone else. To our horror we saw him standing there watering the garden right in front of the window where the customers were trying to have their lunch. It didn't bother him that he had an audience! He didn't think he could wait until he got to the bathroom!

We finally arrived at our campground and managed to get the tents up. One of the events we had planned was a park that had rides. This was perfect because we could pay the admission for the children and let them run all day to their hearts content. We divided them in small groups and had check-in times where they would meet us. With one of the check-ins, we noticed that the boys had won all kinds of stuffed animals. This caused a red flag to go up! How did they win all those prizes with no money? It was time to go back to camp and straighten this mess out. After interviewing each boy separately, we finally pieced the story together and found out that two boys had staged a fight. When the owner of the booth jumped over his booth to break up the fight, two of the boys jumped over the counter and stole the moneybox.

The next problem was to find out what happened to the money! Everyone had a different story. We couldn't get the truth out of any of them! We were convinced that they would sneak out in the middle of the night and try to recover the money. We parents thought we would outsmart them this time. Well we waited all night for them to prowl out of their tents, but they ended up having a good sleep while we hovered around the campground like detectives. When the boys woke up the next morning they were ready to go, and we wanted to get some sleep! It was time to cook breakfast for nineteen people. The next day we took the boys to the police station hoping that they would scare the boys and make them realize how serious this whole thing was. We were told that they were too young to be put in jail, and the police could do nothing. We went to the park and asked the park if they would take action against the boys. We wanted them to learn a lesson. They told us to leave, and that they didn't want to be bothered. For lack of a better consequence, some of the boys wrote multiple lines saying they would never steal again. We have been told by one boy, who has now grown up and has his own family, he believes this is one reason why he never ended up stealing again.

Getting back to regular routine meant back to washing fifteen loads a week and organizing and implementing the chore list, this took about fifteen minutes a day for each boy. Personal hygiene was a problem. Several of the boys had wetting problems and had to shower every day besides washing out their sheets. Sadly enough, we found out that many of the boys did not know how to work the shower. For some reason, they would turn the hot or cold on but didn't know how to turn them together. Perhaps this was why showers were a dreaded event. When one of the boys would come out of his shower, he often didn't smell any cleaner than before. Eventually with teaching and patience, we got the shower problem under control.

Chapter 10

A Child of Our Own?

"...thy children like olive plants round about thy table." - Psalm 128:3b

     This verse rang through my head after our supper prayer. I sat looking around the table at my seven boys and felt so blessed to have my family to care for. I excused myself from the table and ran to my quiet haven, my bedroom. With tears, I thanked our dear Lord for my beautiful family. There was only one thing missing. Although I was a mother, my children were always saying goodbye. I had many tears hugging them for the last time, as they would move either home or elsewhere. I wanted a baby of my own! I knew God had heard my cry.

     We decided to put our names in for adoption. We were told it could be a two-year wait so we knew it wouldn't be anytime soon. We told the social worker we would like a mixed racial baby since we were a mixed racial couple. About six months after we had applied, we received an exciting phone call. The social worker said, "We have a two-month-old boy available. Do you want him?" We didn't have to hesitate. We said, "Yes we would like to see him tomorrow, and bring him home day after." Because of our familiarity with pre-placement visits with fostering, we felt we would be better prepared by doing it this way rather than bringing him home the same day.

That next morning we went to visit the foster home where we saw the cutest brown eyed baby we had ever seen. We held him and spoke to the foster parents. They told us how bright and alert he was. He got very excited when he would hear music, waving his arms and laughing. We were so excited we could hardly wait for the next day to come. We shopped and tried to imagine all that a baby would need. That evening, lying in bed, listening to my husband falling into a deep sleep, and having my usual conversation with God, I knew something was wrong. I felt it in the pit of my stomach, and somehow knew that there was something that was about to go wrong. I woke my husband up and shared my concern with him, and he told me to quit worrying and go to sleep. After a restless sleep, we were awakened by the phone ringing. These words came through the phone line, "I'm sorry Mrs. Taylor, but the mother will not sign the papers, so the baby is not adoptable." I stopped breathing for a few seconds as I tried to comprehend what was going on. We did our best to console each other. We hadn't told anyone about this, because we were planning to surprise our families. There was not complete closure, so we continued to hope and pray the situation would change. God truly was our comfort in those days and we knew we could trust Him. Little did we know how this would all work out in the future!

Life continued in our busy group home. It was good I was busy, to keep my mind off the baby. My husband announced one morning that he would have to leave for a couple of days. We had some out-of-town business that needed to be done. We sat down and talked about how I would manage the boys in his absence. He told me not to ever touch or grab the boys if they were spiralling out of control because if I did, they would probably lash out at me and physically injure me. He called each one aside, and told each boy that he had a special job for him to do. He made each one believe that they were in charge of the house while he was away, and they were to protect me if a fight broke out. He told each one, "I want a report when I get home. Don't tell the other boys you are in charge because if they know they will give you a hard time." They were all on their best behaviour keeping it a big secret, as each one believed that they were in charge. My next few days went very well as they were all extremely co-operative and protective of me. Glenn finally arrived home and was so pleased with the boys we took them to a show to reward them.

A few nights later, we were sitting in the living room just visiting with the boys when something big and black flew over my head. With a blood-curdling scream, I dashed into the kitchen and hid in our walk-in closet. I was trembling at the sight of that ugly bird. My husband finally announced it was just a bat that had come down the chimney. He disposed of it, the coast was clear and I could finally come out of my hiding place!

The next day was a beautiful sunny day. We never knew from day to day what the day would hold. This particular day we noticed the boys were being especially quiet. They were mumbling in low tones to each other and we watched them out of the corner of our eye to see what would transpire next. Suddenly the oldest of the boys came over to Glenn, and said the boys wanted to play fight with him, the only catch was they all wanted to jump him. It would be seven against one. Since two of the boys were six feet tall already, Glenn knew that if this were to take place he would be in trouble. He also knew that if he didn't oblige them, they would think he was scared, and that would give them the power they wanted. Before I knew what was happening they were moving furniture out of my dining room to make room for the fight that was about to take place. The boys stood around the outside of the room and Glenn was in the middle. The look in their eyes showed that they couldn't wait for the fight to begin. Glenn told them, "I have my eye on one of you and I am not going to be responsible for any damages." Everyone backed off and before we knew it, the fight fizzled out. We wouldn't handle the situation quite like this today but it worked at the time while we were young and inexperienced house parents.

From day to day, we asked for wisdom from the Lord on how to handle our new family. We learned from all of these experiences. Little did we know that all of these tough experiences were preparing us for the future the Lord had for us.

Chapter 11

A Birthday to Remember - Then Goodbye

It was my birthday and you won't believe which appointment I booked on my birthday! You'd think an appointment to the spa or a massage, but no - a trip to the dentist. I had not planned it that way- but sometimes my scheduling got right out of hand. This was one of those days!

Since going to the dentist was one of my greatest fears, it was ridiculous that I was sitting in the dentist chair on my birthday. Before I knew it, the dentist walked in and had a look at my mouth. He then proceeded to ask me, "Wendy would you mind being a guinea pig for us today? We have something new we'd like to try on you. It is a gas that you would breathe in and it will make you more comfortable as we fill your tooth." I was very agreeable, as I was game for anything that would make me more comfortable.

Within a few minutes, I was floating across the room. I heard voices, but even they were bouncing. I thought to myself, "I wonder if this is what it is like to take drugs and have a high?" Suddenly he told me he was through and they would be pumping in oxygen. Next thing I knew, my head was feeling funny, and then I started to laugh hysterically. I could hardly walk, I laughed so hard. The dentist seemed quite concerned about me. He told me to have a seat in the waiting room, and not drive just yet. I found a seat in the busy waiting room, holding my sides as I continued to laugh. I was quite embarrassed as the other patients watched me. All of the sudden I saw the dentist stick his head around the corner. His beard, sideburns, and long hair made him look like a baboon to me. Of course I had a little help with the gas I had been given. I started to laugh even harder. My face was hurting and I could not get a hold of myself.

Finally after thoroughly embarrassing myself, I thought I had better drive home. On the way home, I saw a friend of mine. I pulled over and waved for her to come to the car. She jumped in the car and looked at me strangely, as I continued to laugh so hard I couldn't talk. I dropped her off in front of her house and went home to recuperate. When I finally came back to earth, I called her to explain my ridiculous behaviour. This truly was a birthday, I will never forget.

After living in the Kitchener area for two years, we felt the Lord leading us to open a treatment facility in the Leamington area, our hometown. We did not know how this was all going to work out, but we felt this was the Lord leading us. We made our plans and decided we would only let the boys know two weeks before we were to leave. We knew from experience that if we were to tell the boys with too much notice it would be a nightmare for all of us. We knew that more often than not, the way the boys would handle this type of move, would be to experience rejection once again. They would then proceed to take their frustrations out on all of us. Sometimes they would punish the family for hurting them one more time.

Because I had no children of my own, I treated these boys as my own. I loved them as my own flesh and blood. We knew it wasn't fair to the program where we worked for us to try to take the boys with us. We wanted to be honourable in starting our own program. We knew that we would have to give up our boys, let them be placed in other group homes and leave. It almost broke my heart, just thinking about it. It was so much different from just leaving a job and moving. Each evening, while my husband fell asleep, I would be lying beside him praying. I thought I was having a heart attack, as the worry was almost consuming me. I knew we would soon have to tell the boys that we were leaving, and each night the pain got more intense. I kept thinking how they would handle this one more rejection.

Finally, the evening came after supper when we had our Bible story time. We told them we had something very important to tell them. We shared with them that God was calling us to open our own treatment home where we could help more children like them. We were brought to tears as we heard the boys say things such as, "We are so thankful you have helped us, and we want to pray that you would be able to help more boys like us."

John, one of our foster boys, said, "Would you help my brother, he is in the Windsor area. I taught him to steal, so we could have enough food to eat." We responded that we did not have any control over which boys would be referred to us. We told them we could pray though. So together, we had prayer. It was truly a moving experience to witness the maturity of the boys.

I noticed another miracle at this time. After we told the boys, a complete peace came over the boys and us. I knew it was all going to be okay. The Holy Spirit was in our home, and the terrifying moments were gone. We were able to hug each boy goodbye as they moved into various group homes. We knew God loved them more than we did. He had his hand on their lives as well as ours!

Chapter 12

New Start

We moved back to our hometown Leamington with a dream and faith in our hearts. We knew that the dream we had could only be accomplished with God opening doors and blessing our efforts. Opening our own treatment program was more than a notion. We had been told by some of our critics, that it was almost impossible to do this because we did not have the educational background in social work. We only had our experience and, most importantly, our faith in God. We knew we wanted to work with children, and when we weighed out the various directions we could go, we felt that beginning our own program we could help the greatest number of children. If we helped other couples do what we had learned to do, so many more children could be reached.

One of the first things we prayed about was a large farm home on the edge of town with lots of bedrooms. We found the ideal home and moved in when we moved into town. Our next step was to pray for foster children to be referred to our program. Since this was our only financial means, we knew we were really stepping out in faith. We approached both children's aid offices and made them aware that we had beds available. We handed out new brochures and business cards praying that we would receive a positive response. It wasn't long before we received a call saying that they had a boy for us, and his name was Raymond. He was the brother of John whom we had in Kitchener. We realized that he was the boy about which we had prayed. How thrilled his brother would be! When Raymond came, he fell in love with us as we did with him. He brought a little trophy that said "to the best foster parents." We enjoyed our new charge. It wasn't long and the phone was ringing again with new foster boys that were being referred. Our home was soon bursting with boys. Five boys soon filled every bedroom.

One evening we received a surprising phone call. It was the Cambridge Children's Aid. The social worker told us she had our little baby that we had seen, and the baby was available for adoption. She asked if we still wanted him. I didn't have to hesitate or ask my husband. I responded, "Absolutely." The arrangements were made that we were to come the next day and pick him up. What a thrill it was, running through Zellers, buying diapers, shirts, blankets and whatever else we thought the baby would need.

The next morning was so exciting. We got an early start and headed towards Cambridge. We were so full of joy and thankfulness to our Lord. When we arrived, the social worker brought our baby to us, and laid him in our arms. We were given a schedule that he was used to keeping, a diaper bag, a full bottle, and a few diapers. He was such a beautiful baby in his yellow outfit. He was now about four months old. We were so proud of our new bundle of joy.

We soon found out we had two families. How would it work with our boys and our baby? We would soon find out. We were adjusting well to our large family. The biggest adjustment I had was that now when the boys went to school, I did not have time off. I was working all the time.

Another evening the phone rang and it wasn't a happy call. The caller on the other end told me that one of our previous foster boys, Jerry had just died in a fire. He had been one of the boys who had moved into a group home when we moved. There had been a fire behind the walls in the insulation. My mind went back to that day when I went into the director's office, and a longhaired youth about fifteen years old, was just sitting there looking very dejected. My thoughts went back to the shocking phone call. Could it be true? When my husband got home that evening, I shared the latest news with him. He was upset as well. Suddenly he said, "I've got to go to the funeral." Because I was taking it quite hard, I didn't think I could go.

When my husband arrived in Kitchener, he was told that all the kids had been outside, when the fire trucks were putting out the fire. Jerry had run into the house to get something and never returned outside. Tragically, he had died of smoke inhalation. When they went into the house, they found a letter beside his bed addressed to us. He had written it the night before he died. The letter went on to tell us that he was getting straight A's in school and he would soon be going home. He thanked us for all we had done for him.
The letter was handed to Glenn at the funeral and his mom and dad announced that Glenn and his wife were the one who turned Jerry's life around. We knew it was the Lord, but it was so kind of his parents.
After the funeral, we reflected on the past few years and realized something. We were aware that we had made many mistakes but the one thing we had done right was to tell these kids about the Lord. They all knew that He desired to have a personal relationship with them and loved them unconditionally. Most of the boys had accepted the Lord as their personal Saviour. We remembered the day Jerry had. That gave us much peace.

Chapter 13

Adjustments

Once our home filled up with children we decided to hire on other couples to help us. Bob and Carolyn were one of our first couples we recruited to be foster parents. Dr. Kent Billinghurst was the psychologist who came twice a month, to teach behavioural techniques that we needed so desperately. We began a private school in a cottage with a teacher who had two students. We knew from our last group home that some children would not fit into a regular school setting. Some were just too fragmented.

We prayed about everything. We asked God's leading each step of the way. One prayer request we had was that we would have a permanent school and office facility. In the morning, we would watch TV and were very encouraged and inspired by the PTL program. It truly strengthened our faith as we watched people exercise their trust in God for impossible situations. We prayed specifically for a school and office but the catch was we had no money to put down. After some time of looking for the right property with these conditions, we purchased a three-acre parcel with a county school on it with no money down. The zoning would have to be changed and, once again, we went to prayer. Our lawyer took the matter to the town counsel and we received word it had passed. Our next challenge was that we needed desks. After praying about desks, we received word that twenty-five school desks were at the school board and they were getting ready to throw them away. Would we be interested in them? On and on God answered our prayers.

One of the first things Glenn did when we opened our own program was to take the boys to Florida. Bob, one of our foster dads, and Glenn packed up the van and headed south with very excited passengers. Most of the boys had never been outside of Windsor so just crossing the border was exciting. The boys were given many car games to play to keep them occupied, everything from counting all the blue trucks to counting cows. The expressions of awe when they saw Disney World for the first time will forever be stamped in Glenn's memory. The trip was going relatively well until they decided to go swimming in the hotel pool with the many seniors. They were constantly splashing, arguing, and pushing each other, which the retirees did not find very relaxing.

Swimming in the ocean was another unforgettable experience. They were told to walk very carefully, when Patrick let out a blood-curdling scream. When he came out of the water, he had blood running down his leg. Glenn quickly took his shirt off and made a tourniquet. Something had really taken a good chunk out of his leg. A trip to the emergency room remedied the problem. By the time they arrived home, there were two exhausted chaperones but five very happy boys.

When the children first arrived in our home, we would assess them and decide which foster home to place them in. We became a receiving home to make it easier to find appropriate placements. We had as many as fifteen couples working for us. We received our referrals through several Children's Aid Societies. They were aware of our Christian based program, and no smoking policy, but the results were so outstanding, that they placed a number of children with us in spite of our rules.

Chapter 14

Sports at Their Worst and Best

I cannot count how many baseball and basketball games I have sat through, watching my boys. What would get tricky is when two of them would be on opposite teams playing each other. Whom would I root for? Since I am not an extremely competitive person, I would just tell them all to play their best. I must share with you one of the funniest games the children and I ever witnessed.

My husband did not mind the odd game of baseball but he was not a real sports nut, like so many guys. One day, Doug, a friend of ours called and said the Christian baseball league in our area was going to have a game. However, for some reason one team would be short several players. Since this was the playoffs, it was an important game. They asked if our church could pull a team together to help. Doug recruited my husband as well as several other men from our church. They had never played together so they knew this would be quite a challenge. Not only did they not have uniforms, the catcher didn't even have a baseball glove! He used his goalie mitt! My husband wore cowboy boots instead of runners! This team sure looked like a ragtag team, especially beside the other professionally dressed team in their uniforms. Well everyone chuckled as they saw the two teams approach. The team with the uniforms was quite confident I am sure, that this opposing team would not be a challenge. Well when the last score was marked on the board, the ragtag team won. They won the championship game and won the trophy! This was not only a shock to all the players but to the audience as well!

Because most of our boys came into our home with very poor self-images, if they were to lose a game or the coach was to reprimand them, it felt devastating to them. Sometimes they would respond in anger and sometimes depression, in other words anger turned inwards. I was constantly reinforcing the point to play their best and that would make me proud. I would find ways of rewarding them like baking their favourite cookies or taking just one out for ice cream while the others were busy and didn't notice. I was always trying to find ways to make them feel special.

One day my slim son Brent thought he would like to try out for the football team in grade eight. We tried to discourage him and told him we thought he was more suited for basketball. He was determined, so we let him make the final decision. Sure enough this one day after school, he went out for his first practice. We saw this huge giant of a guy walk out, only to discover, this was his coach. One of the first drills the coach had the players do was these boys were all to run toward him and tackle him. Well it was like running into a cement wall. When my son saw this hulk of a man standing there with his legs spread apart, he had a different plan. He came running at top speed towards the coach and just when he reached him, he dove between his legs. The coach was surprised to say the least, and that was the last he saw of my son. My son decided after all that football wasn't for him after all.

Another game I spent many hours watching was basketball. One evening my mother, sister, daughter, niece, and I thought we would watch one of the games. My sister and I got so excited. We kind of lost control and were getting quite loud as we rooted for our favourite team. Our kids kept telling us to keep it down, but we ignored them and kept laughing and just being silly. All of the sudden we turned around to say something to our kids and noticed they had moved. We never felt like we were too old to have fun, I think our kids appreciated that, although they were always trying to tame us down. This happened especially when my sister and I were together.

One basketball game will always be etched in my memory. This particular game I had borrowed my sisters video camera. Since there was talk of my son being recruited into a college basketball team, I felt that we needed to get a video of him playing. Well I had never operated a video camera before but with a few simple instructions, I didn't feel it could be too difficult. The one thing no one told me was that the camera had a microphone on it. As I was watching the game through the eye of the camera, I was narrating all my comments throughout the game. This particular game, I felt the coach was not being fair to my son. I was making comments like, "Just because my son is scoring so many points it doesn't mean you have to take him off the court." and "This is so unfair!" I was being such a mother! Well I was being quite a reporter throughout the whole game. When the game was over my son came up to me and asked if I would let him have the tape, so that he could watch it with the whole team. Apparently, I was the only one who had taped the whole game and the coach wanted to review the game with the boys. You can imagine the laughs when they heard my narrating and I would be shouting, "Pass my son the ball!" It wasn't until my son got home and told me about my narrating that I realized I had been taped. How embarrassing! I wonder why my son never asked for another tape to show his team. I did learn a lesson. I needed to learn to be careful what I say. You never know who is listening.

Chapter 15

Taking a Stand

One day, Joel, one of our fifteen-year-olds, came home and said that for his English project he was to premeditate a murder, and send the essay in for marks. I could not believe this. Immediately I knew something had to be done about this. Joel's brother was in jail for murder, and he was a very angry boy who had grown up without a father. I went to his teacher and tried to have the assignment changed for the class, but the teacher refused to change it. He did allow Joel to have another topic to write his essay on, but it was disappointing that the other students had to carry through with this project.

It wasn't long after that this same English teacher had the class reading a novel with a lot of profanity in it. I had more than one child in his class and they were extremely uncomfortable with this. Once again I had a meeting with the teacher and he informed me that he had no knowledge of the content of the books that he ordered by title. Well I asked him if I could get a group of parents together to go through books and let the school know our opinions and give them some input regarding the content of the books. He was ok with this, so I organized a committee for parents to read these English novels and we continued this for the remainder of years my foster children were in high school.

It was hard to believe this cute little Jim could be such a challenge. When he came to us, he looked like a cute little ten-year-old with long brown bangs hanging in his eyes. He had a great sense of humour and was a lot of fun. When reading his history we found that he and his brother had taken a beer bottle and beat up his mother's boyfriend putting him in intensive care. Apparently, this boyfriend was very abusive and Jim could not stand by and watch any longer.
This one beautiful day I received a call from the school saying that Jim had a problem and I needed to come right away. When I arrived at the school, I noticed that there were five police cars at the school. When I went to the office, I was ushered into a classroom where Jim was sitting with handcuffs on surrounded by five big policemen. He was so small sitting on that chair and surrounded by these police in uniform. I was told he had kicked one of the teachers in the groin when the male teacher had tried to calm him down while having an argument with another student. After sitting for a couple of hours and calming down I was told I could bring him home. He was suspended for a couple of weeks and after many chores and extra schoolwork, he was able to return to school.

It made me realize that old saying "You can't judge a book by its cover" has some real meaning. So often, we are quick to judge others by the way we see them but we don't know their heart.

That next Friday we had another sixteen-year-old boy move in. Jason was quite a thin and rather frail looking boy. He did not have the stamina to play outdoors with the other boys. Sunday we took him to church and following the service there was an alter call. The pastor said if anyone would like to receive the Lord as their personal Saviour they could come forward. Jason went forward and was so at peace and happy on our way home from church. The following day he was feeling very sick so we took him into emergency at the hospital. Later that day he died of a heart attack. We were so thankful that Jason had made his peace with God and was ready to go home to meet his Saviour.

Chapter 16

Sometimes Humorous - Sometimes Not

Teens have an uncanny way of going into the shower and using up all the hot water, spending at least half an hour in the shower and then they innocently comment, "I was just taking a shower." It's hard to imagine how anyone could go through shampoo so fast and take so long in the bathroom. You would think this was their favourite room in the house!

One of our boys named Abe hated to take showers. He was a rather unusual teenager but with coaxing, we would eventually get him into the shower. After some resistance, he finally closed the door to the bathroom with towel in hand. This particular day we noticed the shower was taking far more time than usual. My husband went into the laundry room and noticed that the pipes were very hot. In fact, they were so hot you would burn yourself if you were to experience water that scalding. My husband quietly went and unlocked the bathroom door only to find Abe lying across the floor with his feet crossed resting them on the toilet. The shower was running, and my husband saw a very surprised Abe, who found his rest cut short! He had a few consequences to deal with but he could not figure out how we figured out what he was up to in the shower.   We found another trick getting teens out of a too prolonged shower is to cut off the hot water. It sure moves them into action!

One day my husband heard a noise outside and it was rather unusual because as far as we knew everyone was inside sleeping. When he went down the steps to the boy's rooms, and checked the boys beds, he found that several of them had climbed out the window and were running around outside. He locked the windows and the doors, and when they were ready to come in, they had to ring the doorbell much to their embarrassment. It was a rather humiliating experience to explain what they were doing outdoors.

It was a beautiful day, a great day for shopping. Everyone was in school this day, which was rather unusual. Many days I had at least one child home who was kicked out of school for some reason. When we arrived in Windsor, we decided to go into the art store where I could pick up art supplies for my budding artists. In the back of the store was a monkey in a cage. Since we were animal lovers, we were quite taken with this little fellow jumping all over his cage. I put my finger in the cage and he put his through and touched my fingers. All of the sudden he snatched my glasses off my nose and into the cage they went. He was jumping around with them making monkey noises. We were so startled. We had a good laugh. Eventually we called the owner of the store and asked for help. I did get my glasses back in one piece but it did help to relieve tension with another good laugh!

It was a busy day with much on my calendar. I wanted to go to a Bible study, and to bake a birthday cake and wash clothes of course! I turned on my oven and, surprisingly, it wasn't working! I automatically called my neighbour, whose name was also Wendy, and said "Wendy, this is Wendy. Could I bake a cake in your oven since mine isn't working? I'll explain everything later." Before she could say anything, I was off the phone. A few minutes later, I was running across the street with my nine by thirteen inch pan. After ringing the doorbell and knocking on the door with no response, I went into her kitchen. I was surprised not to see her in the kitchen since I had just spoken to her. I also noticed that the oven had not been turned on yet. I put the cake in the oven and went to leave the house when Wendy came down the steps with a surprised look on her face. I said, "Thank you so much, I'll explain everything later." With that, I left the house.

When arriving at the Bible study with a friend, I barely got into the house when one of the ladies said to me, "Wendy what are you doing here?" I thought it was rather rude to ask, as everyone was invited to the Bible study.

She went on to explain that I had called someone at the other end of the city and asked her to turn her oven on for a Birthday cake that I would be bringing over. She had her oven going for over an hour. I stood in shock as I realized the stupid mistake I had made. Next, I found myself calling both women and explaining. Wendy was called with an apology, she accepted it very well, and Pam was called to tell her that her oven could be turned off because I didn't even know I called her. The ladies all had a good laugh and I once again had another humble pill with which I seemed to be overdosing!

Chapter 17

Girls Another Story

We have often been asked, "Why haven't you taken girls?" The answer to that question is, "We have taken a few girls. We found them more difficult than the boys." We honestly felt more comfortable with boys and perhaps after telling you about a few of our experiences you will understand why. From our experience, we have found that boys will act out their problems when they are troubled about something, but girls will hold them in and their pain and frustration will come out in various ways. The girls were more emotional, and when you add puberty to the mix, it could get more than a little challenging. I believe this is true especially with the type of children we took in, mostly abused, and very fragmented children.

Mary was not afraid of anyone, including boys, teachers, and foster parents. She was a tough looking fifteen-year-old girl with bleached blond hair. She lifted weights, and kept the boys at school afraid of her. I was constantly trying to make her look more feminine, so for church I bought her a beautiful pink dress, nylons, and high heels. I practiced walking with her at home and taught her how to walk like a lady in her high heels. She never mastered it completely.

That following Sunday we walked into church together. Mary started mounting the steps when her heel caught on a step and she came crashing down. Her dress flew up over her head and she landed in a heap on the bottom of the steps. There were several boys standing at the bottom of the steps who saw the whole episode. They grinned and before they knew what happened, Mary had her fists in their faces, daring them to laugh. After that, I felt it was almost hopeless trying to make a lady of her.

Mary had a serious drug problem as well. Every time she came home from a visit, she had to be checked to see if she was carrying drugs back in the house. She would sometimes threaten me and say such things as, "I bet if your husband wasn't here to protect you, you'd be afraid to tell me what to do." She would also threaten to hurt me next time my husband would go away.

Jerry also lived with us at the same time Mary did. She was another very angry girl. She was very angry with her mother and would often take this anger out on me. A few times, I found letters lying around beside my phone, saying that Jerry was going to kill my baby and hurt me as soon as she had a chance. My husband and I didn't take the threats seriously, although today we would think differently about that. We trusted God for protection and moved forward. One day Jerry pulled a complete tantrum. She threw things, and was swearing and was completely out of control. My husband told her to go to her room. Instead of going to her room, she ran out the front door. He ran after her trying to reason with her, and bring her back into the house. There were workmen working outside tarring the sidewalk. She came screaming out of the house.

The workmen put their shovels down, as my husband tried to explain what was going on. Jerry decided not to come home for the next week. She slept at the park or under a tree in our backyard. We continually called her social worker, asking the children's aid to pick her up because she wouldn't let us near her. She was causing so much trouble in the neighbourhood. She would knock on doors begging for something to eat and telling the neighbours, we wouldn't feed her. She even knocked on my parent's door, begging for food. Because she was a foster child, people tended to believe her. We tried to talk to her on numerous occasions but she refused to talk to us.

One day the phone rang and her social worker was on the phone. She said Jerry's dad was coming to pick her up and move to British Columbia. That evening he picked her up and brought her to our home. She told her dad how terrible we treated her. He listened intently to both sides. When we all finished he commented, "I believe Glenn and Wendy have loved you and cared for you. I just want to know why, since you have been so ungrateful and undeserving."

We went on to explain that because of the love we had in our hearts from the Lord, we were able to love her unconditionally. We told him how we had been called to work with children and how God strengthened us and enabled us. He wanted to know more of our relationship with Jesus Christ. We went on to explain how Jesus came to this earth as a baby, lived on this earth for thirty-three years and willingly gave himself up to die on a cruel cross. He did this so that our sins could be forgiven by believing in Him and asking for forgiveness. We could be born in his family. He had tears in his eyes, and he was visibly touched. We sent a Bible with him and said goodbye. About a week later, we received a call from British Columbia. He had walked into a hotel for lunch and there was a Christian Businessmen's luncheon going on. He went and sat down and when the speaker had an alter call, he gave his heart to the Lord and asked forgiveness. He called to tell us he had peace, and had finally found what he was looking for. Since then, we have not heard from Jerry, or her dad, but we know God has them in his care. Entrusting people into His care became a way of life for me.

Chapter 18

Special Surprise

One day the phone rang and it ended up being one of the greatest blessings of my life. The Chatham Children's Aid called to tell us they had a baby girl for us to adopt. We had our son Brent who was now four years old and five teen-age foster boys. We knew this would be challenging but we were so excited about having our own girl. We took Brent to the Children's Aid with us to get her. It was such an exciting time in our life.

Our little three-month-old girl was named Alysha. She really was a one-of-a-kind baby. I used to hear mothers talk of their children being little angels and not getting into things. After our active Brent, I didn't think that there really were children like that out there. I actually thought that all mothers who said such things were lying. Alysha proved me wrong. I could actually put her beside me on the bed with a few toys, lie beside her, and drift off to sleep while she played. When I woke up, she would be sitting there right beside me. I remember one time the phone rang and she was trying to ask me a question. I told her to sit on the step and wait for me to finish my conversation. Forty-five minutes later, I found her still sitting there. When I asked her why she was just sitting there, she told me she was sitting there because I told her to sit there when I was on the phone. I had totally forgotten.

She was a very feminine sweet girl who loved to dress up with dresses and matching barrettes and bows for her hair. She was very innocent and trusting. We felt very protective towards her, with all the foster boys. We didn't let her out of our sight. Most of the boys felt very protective towards her as well, and were very good to her.

When Alysha and Brent would go shopping with me, we would always play a little game. Because I am rather "geographically challenged" as my husband would say, finding my car was always a difficult feat. I would ask the children, "Who can find mommy's car first?" They would both try to be first and of course would lead me to the car. It was not until they were much older that they finally realized that mommy didn't know where the car was! Alysha ended up, along with her brother, working in the public school program with difficult children. She had a natural ability with children. Today she helps in church ministry and is a happily married young lady who looks forward to having her own family one-day.

Frequently I was asked to share my personal testimony at ladies meetings. This one particular meeting I remember during lunch that I had forgotten my notes. Since I was the guest speaker and singer, I rummaged through my big purse looking for my music. I couldn't believe it but I had also forgotten my background tape! I wrote a few notes down on a scrap paper that would have to do for my outline for speaking. I decided to sing a cappella since I knew my music fairly well. When I stood up to speak and sing, I noticed, everything was looking very hazy. It happened after I put my glasses on. Usually I would wear my contact lenses, and then wear reading glasses over them to see the words. When I took my glasses off, I realized they were bifocals that were not mine. By this time, I was standing in front of everyone. I figured I might as well have everyone laugh with me, rather than at me, so I shared my fiasco.

I found out later that the night before I had taken glasses that belonged to the pastor's wife of the church I was speaking at the night before. They looked much like mine and I left her mine. She got a good laugh from it as I did. God sure had a way of keeping me humble. I guess I shouldn't blame these ridicules things on Him. I think that sometimes, I would be so stressed out from my lifestyle that I would forget and do silly things.

I remember one weekend I decided to take a break from everyone and go visit my cousin Audrey. I decided to call home to see how everyone was doing. My five-year-old son Brent answered the phone and when I asked him how everything was, he told me that dad was outside talking to the police. When I asked what happened he told me the boys had stolen all the neighbour's bikes and ran away with them. It hit me like a ton of bricks that my life was so far from normal. I didn't realize it when I was in the midst of the turmoil because we were always trying to cope. I knew my life was in God's hands, and that he would help us get through everything he allowed us to go through. My trust was securely in God.

Chapter 19

More Stress Filled Days!

There were constant challenges having our own program. Every time a foster parent would have a problem, they would call on Glenn. We encouraged them to call when there was a need, because things could get completely out of hand very quickly. For example, a teen-age boy had his foster dad on the floor in a headlock while the whole family stood by. Another time, an eight-year-old boy locked himself in the car and when we arrived on the scene, the car was surrounded by police trying to coax him out of the car.

One day we received a call from a social worker who had a boy in the Windsor jail. He had raped a female guard and tried to smother someone with a pillow. We prayed about this as we always did and felt that the Lord wanted us to take him. He was a

250-pound boy who was mentally challenged. One day my husband took him and several of the boys to the park. They were playing catch, and just having fun. When it was time to go home they raced to the car. They took off running at top speed. When Sam was the last one to arrive at the car, he pulled a temper fit. He started swearing, jumped on Jim, and started pounding him. When Glenn pulled Sam off the younger boy, he bit my husband, drawing blood. Glenn restrained him on the ground while one of the boys went to a neighbour's house and called the police. When the police arrived, he said to Glenn, "I can handle this now." He told Sam to get up and the next thing he knew Sam knocked his hat off and kicked the side of the police car, until he dented it. The police finally needed Glenn's assistance, to get handcuffs on him, and get him into the police car. He was then taken to the town jail, while Glenn went to the hospital for a tetanus shot. Later that day, we received a call from the police station asking if Glenn would mind escorting the young man to Windsor, to the psychiatric ward at one of the hospitals. Glenn along with another foster boy drove him to Windsor, which was about thirty miles away. God protected once again!

One of the boys who lived with us was such a kind-hearted boy. He fit into our family so well. We would have liked to keep him for a long time. Because he was doing so well, and had adjusted so well, the Children's Aid didn't want to leave him with us, for too long. They made plans to move him in with his eighteen-year-old homosexual brother who lived with his friends. At nights, his brother was a stripper. This was considered a stable home to move him into! Sometimes these kinds of decisions were hard for us to take, but our opinions were not even asked, let alone considered.

One thing that was very difficult was that some of the foster children would get very jealous of my children. Because they weren't invited to birthday parties as other children often were, they would sometimes try to sabotage relationships my children would have with their friends.

We had to be careful what we discussed in the house or in the car. If we discussed finances or anything of a personal nature, you could be sure that details would be passed on to teachers, social workers and folks at church. People at church were often the most critical of our parenting. This was because we had to maintain very strict rules to stay in control. The children tended to get bolder away from home. They thought the rules would change, when they were not at home. It didn't take long to figure out that Christian people were often very sympathetic to their situations. Long detailed often-exaggerated stories would be told by our foster children. One of the things we insisted on was that certain children would have to stay within range of where we could see them. If not bullying younger children, they could easily abuse a younger or weaker child. Because the children looked normal, and seemed very normal to talk to, people often miscalculated them.

Many Christmases we would get calls from social workers telling us that families did not want their children home for Christmas. How do you tell a child, "Mom and dad don't want you home for Christmas?" We would go Christmas shopping and try to excite the children about special events and surprises we would have over the holidays. Usually the children that were left behind were the more difficult disruptive children. Because of this factor, and it being such an emotional time of year, we would often decide to have our own family Christmas. I have to admit there were a few Christmas's, that I felt sorry for us, because we could not join the rest of our families for big turkey dinners. We knew that bringing several of our difficult boys could ruin everyone's Christmas. When we did join in, we would leave early. At home, the children knew their boundaries and we didn't worry about things being broken or stolen. Fights could easily break out with other boys, or even cousins. We tried to make this as fun a time as possible with our own celebration.

With all this going on in our everyday life experiences, we realized we needed more prayer. I started a telephone prayer chain that prayed for not only the needs of our family, but also any needs that were called in. This chain has been going for ten years and literally hundreds of people have been involved with the prayer Connection. Thousands of requests have been lifted up in prayer, and so many answers to prayer. We saw many miracles take place and we are confident that the protection my children, husband, and I experienced during this time in our lives was a result of prayer.

Chapter 20

Almost Enough

For about ten years, we were running our own treatment program. It got to the point where I was burning out badly. I think I was past the point of burnout and didn't even know how exhausted I was. I realized that everything was bothering me and I could hardly distinguish between big and little problems.

One beautiful sunny day after everyone went to school, I thought I would do my grocery shopping. I ended up with two shopping carts full as usual and drove home dreading the mammoth job ahead of me, carrying in all the groceries and then putting them all away. I managed to get them on the counters when suddenly I felt completely overwhelmed. I did not know where to put all the groceries. I started to cry. I went to my bedroom, lay down, and called my husband. I knew I was in trouble, I just didn't know how bad it was.

We decided I needed to see a counsellor. I was quite hesitant at first, but I knew I needed help. I started sharing my life story with him and he told me I needed to take a stress test. The first thing I noticed was that I could not remember what the date or year was. I was so panicky about this that I ran all over the office looking for a calendar so I could figure out what year it was. He had left me in the office for a time to work on my test. When he came back, I told him I had been looking for a calendar and had not found one. He was quite calm and not upset with me as I had expected he would be. I'm not sure why I thought he would be angry or upset with me. After he marked the test, he said that my husband needed to hear the results. He told us both that I had four flat tires and nowhere else to go. He told us that if we didn't take a break in working with children, that I would end up being a very sick lady with the possibility of being hospitalized. He told my husband that he had a choice to make. He told him it was either the business or me. I sat with bated breath waiting for my husband's response. He said, "I choose my wife of course." It pained me as I thought of my husband's dream that he was being forced to abandon. He wanted to start programs like ours all over Canada. The Counsellor went on to tell us that I needed to move out of the country for about a year. That was impossible financially, so we went to Florida for one month, sold the business, and moved to Mississauga.

After a few months of rest, I decided I needed something to do. I applied for a private nursing position. I received a call shortly after, asking me if I would be interested in looking after a ninety-one-year-old lady. This older lady was in a nursing home and was such a challenge that the nurses refused to care for her, unless she had her own private nurse. Jo Anne was definitely a challenge but after taking in so many difficult teen-age boys, it was a relief to be able to care for someone, and go home to a quite house at the end of the day. She begged me not to leave, when we decided to move. Shortly after we moved, I heard she passed away.

After working with Jo Anne, I began to get restless, wanting to have children again. We went to probation services in Toronto inquiring about the possibility of us taking in several boys. With the experience we had we were called shortly afterwards. Two boys, fourteen and fifteen-year-olds, were given us. They had been involved in crimes and sentenced to open custody. We were to read them their rights if they did not come home from school promptly or if they left the house without permission. Over the next few years, we continued to take probation kids and found them much easier than the children's aid kids. They knew that if they didn't toe the line they would be locked up in a detention home somewhere. Many of them, once their environment changed, settled right down.

Many of our boys went on to lead productive lives but a few were destined for trouble. Some of the boys had been so severely abused and neglected that the short time we had them was not enough time to change their lives. Before you could even build on their lives, much of their former lives had to be eradicated. Some of our boys ended up going to jail. Sunday afternoons we would often take Brent and Alysha to the closest jail where some of the kids were serving time. We would visit them and try to leave them some words of hope and encouragement. Slowly we were getting somewhat involved again. It was hard to cut out this part of our lives, when we had spent so many years with children. We knew God was in control of our future and although we could not see up the road, we trusted him to take us the rest of the way.

Chapter 21

Another Challenge!

This time when the phone rang, the social worker was offering us an eight-year-old with a fiery temper to go along with his red hair. Little Derek was a very manipulative child who had destroyed his parents second marriage by playing in between them. After settling into our home, he was asked on this particular day to tidy the shoes in the garage. Since we had a large family of boys, our garage would sometimes look like a shoe factory with every kind of running shoe possible. The challenge came when you tried to find a matching pair because nobody took the time to line up their shoes. When Derek saw the mess, he pulled a temper tantrum. Instead of doing what he was told, he threw the shoes all over the garage making an even worse mess. My husband was not too pleased with him to say the least. Glenn went into the garage and picked Derek up, and sat him on the freezer. He then looked him straight in the eyes and told him in a firm voice that he would be picking all the shoes up and that he would not be doing that again. Derek screamed obscenities at Glenn, and refused to do what he was told. He was then put in a time out area until he settled down. He finally co-operated and straightened the garage out.

As far as we were concerned, the incident was over. It wasn't in Derek's mind. The next morning he went to his specialized school for behavioural children. He went to one of the counsellors at the school and reported last night's incident with his own twist to the story. His counsellor took notes and especially the part where he was frightened of his foster dad.

A few days later, we were called by the Children's Aid to come for a routine meeting. When we arrived, we were ushered into a room with fifteen social workers, supervisors, counsellors, teachers and anyone that had anything at all to do with Derek. Each person had their say as they went around the room, about Derek and this incident in the garage. Most of them said Derek was afraid of Glenn and that he had done nothing wrong to initiate the incident. The outcome of this "court case" was not looking very favourable for us. We were in total shock as we heard the reports of the counsellors and teachers who all were ready to nail us to the wall, and believe the child rather than us. We thought we had a positive working relationship with these people.

After hearing the testimonies of all these people sharing, we were finally given an opportunity to defend ourselves. We told the group that we had a very positive relationship with Derek, and that this was a one-time incident. We stated that we honestly didn't think we had done anything wrong. We felt he was trying to get even with us, because he had to clean up the mess and didn't want to.

Finally, the moderator wrapped up the meeting by telling the group that he had known us for twenty years and in all his years of working with us, he had never had a child come back and complain of mistreatment. He concluded that we had helped many children, and he believed our story. We were set free to go and the meeting was dismissed. We knew God had vindicated us once again. What an answer to prayer!

On another occasion, we were called to come for another meeting. I have to admit, after what had happened we were a bit leery of meetings. This time, we were to answer questions that a team of social workers would ask us. They gave us different behavioural scenarios that children could act out, and then we were to tell them how we would handle the various situations. After about an hour of questioning, they asked us what behavioural technique we were most often using. We told them that we prayed about every situation and God would give us the remedy for the various problems. They seemed in awe of our answers and were very complementary to us. They told us we were just being modest and that they really did want to know how we knew the answers to working with these difficult children. We knew the source of any wisdom that we had, and it certainly was not us. Once again, we were so thankful to our dear Lord for giving us wisdom when we ask him, just as he promised in his word.

Chapter 22

The Last of My Children!

We received a call saying there was an emergency placement for a nine-year-old boy. His mom and stepdad had told him that they were taking him camping and he and his sister were to pack their clothes. Next thing the children knew they were dropped off at the Children's Aid society. Paul was then taken to our home where he was told he would only be for a few days. Every day he would look out the window for his mom and dad to come and pick him up. He cried and cried day and night. At night, he would have nightmares. Sometimes in the middle of the night, I would awaken to noises. When I would go into his room, I would quite often find him crying and my son Brent, who was four years older than him, would have his arm around him, trying to comfort him in his own childlike way.

We grew to love little Paul, although he was quite a handful sometimes. He found school quite challenging because of his learning disabilities. He was a very clever and lovable boy. He had quite an attachment to his things, which was typical of children that had been traumatized in relationships in their early years. Paul had a real problem with his temper. He would get agitated very easily and have severe temper tantrums that would often result in fights at school. When his parents didn't come back for him, the days turned into weeks and then months. After about a year we received a phone call from his mother one day and she said we were doing a better job raising him then she could, so she wanted us to raise him until he was old enough to be independent. He continued to have occasional visits with her but seemed more confused and upset than ever after the visits. His social worker tried to get him into counselling but to no avail. He refused to get counselling from anyone but us. One day his social worker came for a visit. Paul was in an exceptionally foul mood. Before anyone knew it, we heard him tell his social worker he was going to kill her. She was terrified and ended up having a nervous breakdown. She got out of social work completely. She told us at this time that she would understand if we chose not to keep him any longer. We told her no way, we were a family and we wanted to stick it out with him. As he grew through the teen-age years, he became increasingly more difficult.

We continued to bring him to the church youth group and did as much counselling with him as we could. One camping experience with the youth had a profound effect on him. He came home a changed boy and released a lot of guilt and pain through prayer. He came back happier than we had ever seen him. Although I believe he was sincere in his newfound faith, he still had a violent streak in him. Months turned into years and one day he went to school and decided to draw a picture of his high school teacher. That wasn't so bad, but the problem was he drew her in the nude. Because he was a very good artist, it was very graphic, and then he threw it on her desk. He had quite a long detention for that incident. He now turned sixteen and was getting more difficult as time went on. One Christmas my family all got together, and Paul had just come back from a visit with his family. We were at the church in the fellowship room having a lovely Christmas dinner together. We had another boy at the time called AP. He was an aggravator like no other. When Paul walked into the room, AP called him a name. Paul doubled up his fist and took a swing at AP, and broke his nose. AP was crying as blood ran down his face. My husband had left the family celebration early, and all the relatives were panicking as each one had different advice what should happen next. The one thing I knew was that I had to get my boys out of there, and settle them down. I told them to both get into the car, and Paul said he was going to do it again. I took AP in the car and I told Paul he would have to walk home, since he was still enraged. I put cold packs on AP's face and waited for Paul to arrive. I kept AP out of sight when Paul walked in. My brother-in-law came and sat in the living room waiting for Paul, as the family was afraid to trust him with me. I was not afraid, I just would have been more confident if my husband had been home. When Paul walked in, he still had a very angry look on his face. He told us he had beaten someone else up on his way home because he was so angry. After settling down AP, and getting him to a doctor, and giving Paul a consequence, life settled down somewhat normally again.

Another Christmas get-together with Paul's family was the straw that broke the camel's back. He came home that next weekend with a strange look in his eyes. When asking him how he enjoyed his visit, he told us that his father had thrown a bag of drugs on the table in front of him. He obviously indulged himself, and was very high. He turned to my daughter and told her he was going to smash her face, next time her parents were gone. She was the same age as him, but she was no match for him physically, as he was becoming a big boy. She was terrified, and we knew something had to change. We could no longer have our daughter living in fear, and this threat was the end of the road. She was already hurrying home after school, and locking herself in our room, if we were not home and she and Paul were the first to arrive. She never knew what his mood would be. We called his social worker, and within a few days, he came, packed up his clothes, and walked Paul out to the car. He was very angry with us, and for spite lit up a cigarette and threw it on the driveway. My heart was broken. I had a good cry, as I prayed for Paul. It was so disappointing to have him leave in this state. He had lived with us for seven years and I had such big dreams for him. I knew my Heavenly Father loved him more than I did, and I knew he would be safe in His arms. We knew he had been taught another way of life, and God would bring to his memory the things he had learned. Now the choices were up to him. Even though we could not physically be with him, we knew our prayers always would.

He was placed in a group home, where he broke the placement down within a few days. He was then placed in his own apartment with enough money for groceries and rent. Since then we have seen him very little but we continue to pray for him. We have had some very positive times with him, but our hearts break for him as he is not happy and his life style is dangerous. We are confident God has His hand on his life, even though we cannot be there to protect him. One day I was sitting in a waiting room in a hospital waiting for my daughter to have some test. The room was empty, and as I sat there, someone came and sat right next to me. I could tell it was a young man, and I was afraid to pull myself away from my magazine to look at the guy. When I finally did, I looked into the eyes of Paul who was grinning at me. He told me he had been standing in the hallway watching me, debating whether to come and speak. The reason he was hesitating, he said, was that I would tell him I was praying for him, and that would make him mad. He said that he had been in a fight the night before in a bar, and his friend had been severely cut by a beer bottle, and was in intensive care. He was on his way to visit him. He had to admit that he knew that the prayers I was praying for him were working.

A year ago his two children, the mother of his children, and Paul came to visit us. We had a wonderful time together as a family. We continue to pray for our lost prodigal son. One day we will be reunited as a family.

Chapter 23

Reuniting with the Past

One day Glenn and I stopped at a favourite coffee shop for a cup of tea. Just as my husband was entering the restaurant a big, bearded, motorcycle guy with tattoos walked up to him and threw his arms around him. As my husband tried to gain his composure this fellow said "Do you remember me Glenn? I'm Sammy, one of your foster boys." Of course, we remembered him. As they talked, Sammy said the two things he remembered most were my cooking and the Bible Stories. He was so happy to meet up with us again. We were happy to see the Bible stories had never left his memory.

One day we were walking through a mall and a young fellow and a young lady were obviously following us. We finally went over to talk to them. After finding out that he was another of our foster boys, he mentioned that he did not have any pictures of himself for several years, while he was in foster care. We were able to go through a few albums and find some pictures for him that he treasured so greatly. He seemed to be doing well looking after his wife and two girls. It was so good to reunite with him.

One day we were having plumbing problems. We called the local plumber and much to our surprise when we opened the door, we recognized the person standing there. Brent was now a plumber and was as surprised to see us, as we were to see him. He was not married but was supporting himself and seemed quite happy. How exciting that reunion was.

One of our most challenging boys by the name of Greg was living out West. It surprised us to find out he was a responsible father and living with his wife and employed. He was a boy I'm afraid no one had much faith in. He had too much baggage in his past. He was only six years old when he came into care and had so much going against him. Prayer changes things, and this was such a blessing to find out.

One beautiful sunny day my husband and I went down to the river to relax. We were sitting there on our lawn chairs and a man came up to us and asked if we were Glenn and Wendy Taylor. We answered him in the affirmative. He told us that His son Timmy had grown up to be a responsible father and was living up north, working in the coalmines. Apparently, his wife was no longer with him but he was raising his girls on his own. This was the little guy who used to be such a runner. We will never forget the day we heard him ask the Lord to come into his life.

We had a boy who found us after searching for ten years for us. He never forgets us on mother's day or father's day and always sees us at Christmas. We have had the privilege of marrying him and counselling him throughout various stages of his life. We still stay in close contact with him.

We went into a restaurant one night for supper. The waitress took one look at us and ended up in a flood of tears. We instantly recognized her as being Terry. She and her sister had been our neighbours in the early years of our marriage. Because her mom was not home much of the time, we took her and her sister in and raised them as our own. They lived in between our home and their mom's home. We loved these little girls and prayed for them regularly. Since we met up with Terry, we frequent whatever restaurant she happens to be working at. We try to keep the communication going between us. She gives us big hugs now, and often walks us out to the car. She keeps asking my husband to take her truck for a drive. This is quite an honour, because it really is her pride and joy. We still are a long way from where we need to go with her, but she is beginning to trust us. She has been so deeply wounded in her life that she leads a very lonely life. We care for her deeply, and feel that God has a purpose in her reuniting with us.

When we opened our small church just a year ago, we were surprised to find out one of our previous foster boys lives across the street. I'm sure this is not a coincidence, although we have not been able to get him out to church yet.

Another fond memory was when rode along with our boys in a float promoting Focus on the Family. We truly could say from the bottom of our hearts, and from experience, how important wholesome families are. We lived with the results of dysfunctional wounded families for many years trying to repair the damage done to the children. I hope that our lives have made a little dent in some way in relieving the pain and suffering so many have experienced.

Although we have given our lives to help the hurting, we know that it is only due to the sacrifice that our dear Lord made for us. What we have sacrificed is nothing in comparison to the price paid for our sin. It is because of Him, it is through Him, and it is His to receive the glory and honour.

Chapter 24

Some Valuable Lessons

As I look back at my 25-year journey, working with many broken and fragmented children it has been such a fulfilling and exciting life. Many lessons have been learned which have made me into the person I am today. I would like to share a few of these lessons with you.

I have learned that God's promises are true. He said He would never leave us or forsake us - I found that to be so true! (Hebrews 15:5)

I have learned that He will keep me in perfect peace when I pull away from the rat race of life and curl up with Him. Isaiah 26:3 "Thou wilt keep him in perfect peace, whose mind is stayed on thee: because he trusteth in thee."

I have learned that "The LORD is my strength and my shield; my heart trusted in him, and I am helped: therefore my heart greatly rejoiceth; and with my song will I praise him." (Psalm 28:7) Even when my heart was broken and I said goodbye one more time to one of my children - God healed my troubled heart and gave me joy again!

Mark 11:25 "And when ye stand praying, forgive, if ye have ought against any: that your Father also which is in heaven may forgive you your trespasses." Many times I have had to forgive these children for the crimes they committed before I could love them. Sometimes it was abusive parents I had to forgive. Only then could my Father forgive me. When I couldn't forgive - I asked Him to forgive through me.

Romans 12:15 "Rejoice with them that do rejoice, and weep with them that weep." Often I would have tears rolling down my face as I listened to the unfair treatment many of my children received. I believe this touched their hearts, as they knew I cared.

Psalm 37:7 "Rest in the LORD, and wait patiently for him." How many times have I waited and waited for God's answer to my prayers. Although He often doesn't answer in my time frame - He does answer right on time. My adopted son was a perfect example.

Psalm 37:4 "Delight thyself also in the LORD: and he shall give thee the desires of thine heart." Although I was unable to have my own children He granted me the desires of my heart. He gave me a family. Now as I look back, the only thing I missed was labour pains but I have the same result! I have loved being a mother after all God made me one!

Psalm 27:1 "The LORD is my light and my salvation; whom shall I fear? the LORD is the strength of my life; of whom shall I be afraid?" There were times when my sixteen-year-old and seventeen-year-old foster boys frightened me. When they threatened to burn our house down while we were sleeping - I had to put my confidence in the Lord. Every time the Lord would give me a peaceful sleep in spite of the threats! He is so faithful.

James 1:5 "If any of you lack wisdom, let him ask of God, that giveth to all men liberally, and upbraideth not; and it shall be given him." Many times I found myself on my knees asking God for wisdom on how to handle various problems. In every case a thought would come on how to remedy the problem. As I look back I do believe many times they were God's thoughts pouring into my mind! I know I was not smart enough to deal with the many problems.

Psalm 55:22 "Cast thy burden upon the LORD, and he shall sustain thee: he shall never suffer the righteous to be moved." Many, many times I placed my burden in his lap and he strengthened me and revived me. He gave me hope and saw me through!

Proverbs 22:6 "Train up a child in the way he should go: and when he is old, he will not depart from it." We raised our own adopted children to fear God, worship, and love Him and today we are reaping the benefits! They love the Lord and are actively involved in Christian ministry. This is the greatest investment of all!

Where We Are Today

My husband Glenn and I live in Leamington, Ontario, Canada. We have left our ministry of working with children on a full time basis. We still stay connected with children through volunteer driving for the Children's Aid society. We teach child-rearing seminars and do some one-on-one counselling with couples who have challenging children.

We have taken on a church in Windsor over this past year that is a church plant named Rose City Community Church. My husband is the pastor, and I wear whichever hat needs to be worn. There are hurting people whom we have grown to love, that God has sent to our church family. We have our health, and are so blessed that God still has opportunities for us. I am writing and planning ladies seminars in future. One is "Who Is Raising Whom?" and the other is a women's seminar called "Becoming Beautiful." The ministry "The Prayer Connection" that I founded fourteen years ago is still vibrant and praying for thousands of requests. Lastly, I am able to spend more time writing, which is a great love of mine. Thanks for taking the time to read my story. I would love to hear your thoughts on my first book.

May God Richly Bless You,

Wendy Taylor

If you would like Wendy to come and speak in your area or to comment on her first book, please contact her at:

Address: P.O. Box 28081
        500 Tec. Rd. E. Windsor, Ont. Canada N8X 5E4
Email: wendytaylor@mdirect.net